Sisters Across the Sea

Adopted by the
Bono of Ghana

ALSO BY AGNES BOATENG

Combined English and Maths

Sisters Across the Sea

Adopted by the Bono of Ghana

Agnes (Abena) Boateng
 Jo (Akosua) Williams

monte ceceri

SISTERS ACROSS THE SEA

Copyright © 2025 by Agnes Boateng and Jo Williams

All rights reserved

On the cover: bone and ivory necklace from the Techiman Market by Jo Williams (2025) and the Ghana flag by Kaufdex (2017, 2697634, Pixabay)

Interior images by the authors and also courtesy of:

Vecteezy: Ghana map by rightmeow2 (no date, 168559)

Pixabay: Benny Coffie (2017, 2717911); Lapping (2016, 1927847 and 1927853); Oladapo Olusola (2017, 2419575); Pernilla Klockars (2017, 2011483); Pixabay (2017, 2424452 and 2870691); Oliver Schmid (2022, 7394094)

Wikimedia Commons: Eggi (1994, GNU FDL); two images by Knowledge and Philosophy (2014, CC-BY-SA-4.0 INTL); Emmanuel Owusu (2013, CC-BY-SA-4.0 INTL); Suyash Dwivedi (2019, CC-BY-SA-4.0 INTL); Tetraeder (1980, GNU FDL)

Savannah Morning News, "Two Jenkins Students Win AFS Scholarships," June 5, 1975, 8D, USA TODAY NETWORK via Imagn Images

The Miriam and Ira D. Wallach Division of Art, Prints and Photographs: Photography Collection, "The Commodore Hotel, New York," The New York Public Library Digital Collections, https://digitalcollections.nypl.org/items/510d47e3-e01d-a3d9-e040-e00a18064a99

Harry Warnecke and Lee Elkins, "Shirley Temple (1938)," National Portrait Gallery, Smithsonian Institution (gift of Elsie M. Warnecke), https://www.si.edu/object/shirley-temple%3Anpg_NPG.94.48

No part of this book may be reproduced, stored in a retrieval system, or transmitted by any means, electronic, mechanical, photocopying, recording, or otherwise, without written permission from the publisher or author, except in the case of brief quotations embodied in critical articles or reviews. For additional information, press inquiries, or bulk or educational purchases, please contact Monte Ceceri Publishers.

Boateng, Agnes, 1956– author, and Williams, Jo, 1958– author
Sisters across the sea: adopted by the Bono of Ghana
ISBN: 978-1-949512-26-7 (paperback)
ISBN: 978-1-949512-27-4 (eBook)
1. Ghana. 2. Foreign study — Ghana. 3. Africa, West.
4. Ghana — History. 5. International cooperation.
6. Female friendship. 7. Autobiography I. Title

Monte Ceceri Publishers
Savannah, GA
www.swanhorse.com
www.montececeri.com

This book is dedicated first to our families. For years, they have listened to stories of our relationship with each other and our adventures. They are happy now to pass the baton and allow us to share these with you.

Next, to the beautiful Ghanaian people, who welcomed us with open arms.

Finally, a special dedication to the descendants of the African families taken from their homes against their will because of the transatlantic slave trade.

It happened before our time, and we all share a part of the story. Remember.

Friendships

Friendships built from the inside out and from the ground up.

Bonds that are made to stand the test of time and emotions.

Much as a mason constructs a wall brick by brick, the mortar is the substance that secures each brick to its place.

Different bricks are placed at certain points, much as other friends are placed in our lives to help support our structure.

The elements of society may pummel against friendships, but true friends will hold their place, becoming even stronger.

After the struggles of life are over, I just want my brick to read:

"A True Friend."

Place my brick in your wall, and together everywhere friends will stand tall.

Remember me, I'm just a friend.

Kaya Xavier Glover
September 21, 2000 – November 7, 2021
Midway, Georgia

Contents

Friendships — vii

The Importance of Tribes and Names — 13

1. A Tale of Two Sisters — 17
2. And Where Is This Ghana? — 23
3. New York — 29
4. Akwaaba Accra — 35
5. Shirley — 47
6. Elmina Castle — 53
7. Kumasi to Sunyani — 59
8. Chiraa — 65
9. Fufu: The Mother Dish — 73
10. Father and Family — 79
11. Girl Talk — 87
12. Culture Shock and Chiefs — 97
13. Northern Jaunts — 109
14. Bredi — 121
15. Coming Together — 127

Acknowledgments — 133
About the Authors — 135

Sisters Across the Sea

Adopted by the Bono of Ghana

The Importance of Tribes and Names

The Brong–Ahafo region in central Ghana was created in 1957, the same year Ghana gained independence from Great Britain. The Bono and Ahafo communities comprising this area are an Akan people, the largest ethnic group in the country. Since 2018, this administrative state has been redrawn as the Bono, Bono East, and Ahafo regions.

This book is, in part, a story of how two girls from very different cultures became sisters. It is a relationship that spans fifty years as of this year (and that sometimes large, sometimes not-so-large idiomatic "pond"!) — a sisterhood made possible because of AFS Intercultural Programs (AFS). Founded in 1915 as the American Ambulance Field Service and active during both World Wars, leaders of this humanitarian effort established a secondary school student exchange program in 1946 intended to perpetuate intercultural understanding in peacetime.

SISTERS ACROSS THE SEA

*Agnes "Abena" Boateng, a neighbor (known as "Superman"),
and Jo "Akosua" Mooney in Chiraa, 1975*

Agnes "Oheneba" Boateng is "a natural-born leader." She is also known as "Abena," which is Twi for a girl born on Tuesday. Both of her names imply a "pioneering spirit." She is determined and courageous, rising above adversity and embracing life's struggles as challenges to overcome. Throughout her years, she has served the needs of communities both near and far.

When Josie Mooney arrived in Chiraa, Ghana, in 1975, Abena and her siblings named her "Akosua Broni"*—Twi for a White girl born on Sunday and an appellation denoting a "radiant soul," a vibrant energy and joyful spirit, and a zest for life shared with those around her.

Though beginning with different names and born to different communities, they are family—forever connected to each other and determined to deepen the bonds of humanity throughout the world.

---

* The term *oborɔnyi* (sometimes transliterated as *oburoni*, *oboroni*, or *obroni*) has many meanings. As poet and African historian Kwabena Akurang-Parry explained in a 2011 online discussion, it may be used as a pejorative or with affection—whether indicating someone who is mischievous, beloved, European, Western, White, biracial, or merely foreign to a region. Ghanaian scholar and statesman J.B. Danquah wrote in 1956 that he had "it on the authority of the late Nana F.W. Akuffo, Omanhene of Akwapim, that the Akan word for horizon is *boro*, and that *oboroni* is derived from it." See Kwabena Akurang-Parry, "Etymology 'Obroni,' 'Brofo': Reply," *Humanities and Social Sciences Online*, June 25, 2011, and J.B. Danquah, "Notes on 'Oburoni' and 'Buronya,'" *Transactions of the Gold Coast and Togoland Historical Society* 2, no. 2 (1956): 71–72.

A Tale of Two Sisters

Akosua

In the tenth grade, I met my first exchange student who was from Austria. She stayed with the Nicholsons, her host family, for an entire school year. This intrigued me — this idea of students swapping families and countries as both amateurs and ambassadors. I tried to engage with her, and we soon became friends. Through her and her host family, I then met a group of Brazilian exchange students and experienced my first Carnivàle (a celebration before Lent similar to Mardi Gras in Louisiana). We sang out loud to Elton John's "Benny and the Jets," and we danced in the street as one, throwing confetti and forming a conga line to the hip-hop music of Brazil.

That's when I knew: I, too, wanted to be an exchange student.

Students Josie Mooney and Patricia Ann Hardy featured in the local paper

In 1975, I applied to the AFS, three copies of my submission all handwritten — copied one from another — because I did not have access to a copy machine. Since I had been taking Spanish for five years, I hoped to become fluent by being placed with a host family in a Spanish-speaking country.

Next came the interview, both with my family and me, about why I wanted to go to another country. I must have done well since, not long after, a letter arrived in the mail.

I was accepted!

But not to a country where Spanish was the lingua franca... I was invited to Ghana. No one in my family even knew where that was. I pulled out the atlas. It was in Africa! My curiosity and excitement grew.

The next letter to arrive was even more interesting — one I cherish to this day and treasure as a keepsake. Written on flimsy blue paper with foreign stamps, it was from Agnes Boateng, soon to be my host sister. She had written to me all the way from a small village in the middle of Ghana, excited about my arrival and describing her large family and homeland in detail.

Gradually, my family warmed to the idea and helped me prepare. My grandma, Mooney, made me a new wardrobe consisting of shorts with matching tops, and other family and friends supplied me with gifts to bring from Georgia. I found myself, then all of seventeen, interviewed by local television stations and newspapers, asking me about my expectations for the upcoming adventure. My knowledge of Africa consisted of what I saw on *Mutual of Omaha's Wild Kingdom* and old black-and-white Tarzan movies. Perhaps not the best background, though most of us understood very little about Africa as a continent and even less about a small country named Ghana.

Agnes "Abena" Boateng reading a newspaper in 1975

Abena

At Sunyani Secondary School, about twenty kilometers from Chiraa, I met Ms. E.H.M. Heskett, a White British woman who was my house mistress. We nicknamed her "Ohe" and ran away whenever we heard the clicking of her wooden stiletto sandals as she walked up and down the stairs. Ms. Heskett was sweet but scary. She ensured that the "naughty" girls, Georgina and Joanna (who might be too vocal or tardy), had their share in cutting the grass — a very unwanted chore at the school.

One fateful Saturday in 1975, Ms. Heskett called me to her office to discuss a yet-to-be-named issue. I panicked and wondered if I had left my bed undone during the week and whether I was going to be punished. I knocked on her door, trepidatious with fear.

"Come in, Agnes," she said, and she offered me a chair.

I breathed a sigh of relief. Chairs and punishments rarely occurred together. If I had crossed some line or failed to adhere to school policy, 'she would've had me stand, then rebuke me and assign me land to weed behind the girls' dormitory.

Instead, she brought out an envelope.

"I received this letter from the U.S. Embassy," she said, "to select two students, one girl and one boy, based on their academic performance and behavior to host students coming from America. And I have selected you and Henry Opoku Ware."

I didn't know Henry, who was a year ahead of me, so I asked Ms. Heskett who he was. Both Henry and I were science students and must have been like turtles within our shells because we didn't know each other after being in the same boarding school for three years!

Ms. Heskett arranged to take me the following weekend to my house in Chiraa to discuss the situation, and its three-month obligation, with my family.

A new adventure for all of us, they were excited to host this yet-to-be-named American student as part of our family.

And Where Is This Ghana?

I was going to Africa!

My family was truly excited for me, but many questions remained...

Where exactly was Ghana?

I dug through our set of *Encyclopedia Britannica* books, locating the volume containing all things "G," and flipped through its pages. An *Atlas of the World* helped as well.

Ghana, in land mass, is about the size of Oregon. There is a five-hour time difference between Savannah and Chiraa because Ghana is located near the prime meridian. While it also is closer to the equator, the weather in June and July is similar to that of Georgia — although the hottest month in Ghana is March, arguably the best time of the year in the American South. A tropical climate, Ghana has sporadic rain showers that are refreshing and cool and tamp down the

Sisters Across the Sea

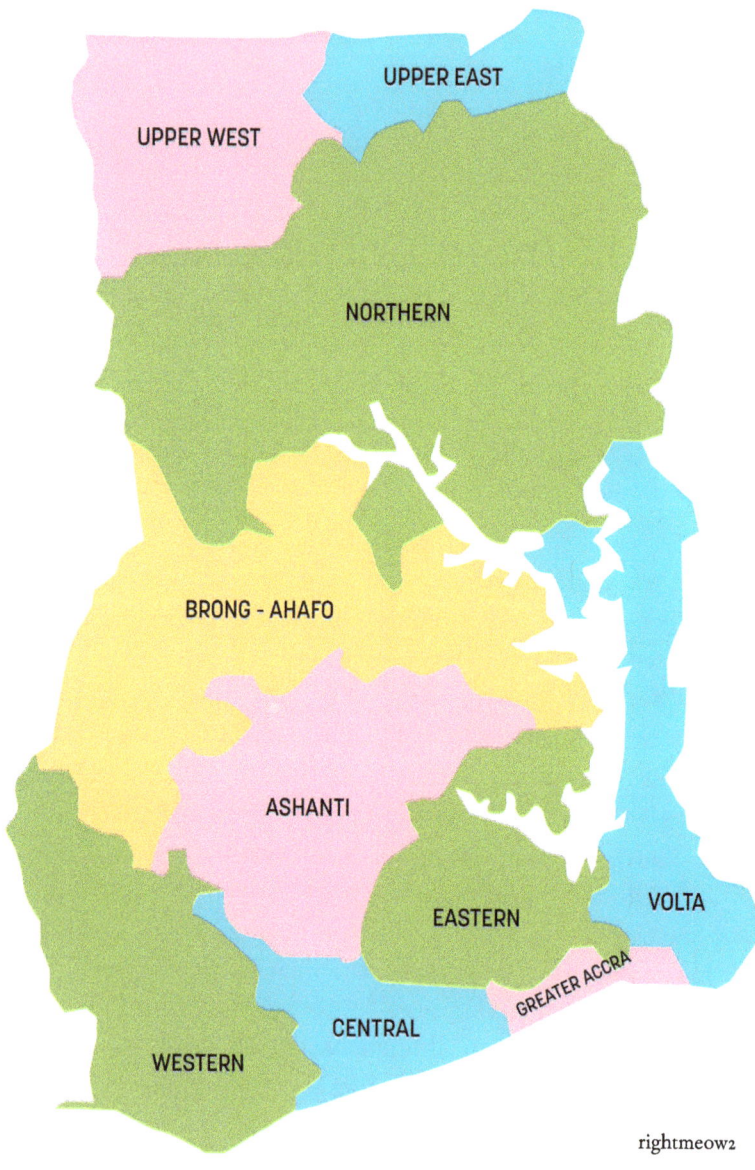

Ghana in 1975. In 2018, the country created six new regions, including redrawing the Brong–Ahafo administrative state as the Bono, Bono East, and Ahafo regions.

dust of the many unpaved roads. Debris caused by the rain is also rinsed off the streets and into the narrow drainage channels that line the paths and lanes.

In the fifteenth century, as both the so-called "Age of Discovery" and transatlantic slave trade began, countries in Europe sought new places to expand. The Portuguese were the first to colonize Ghana in the late 1400s. Ghana's location and resources were deemed optimal for trading, particularly its gold reserves. During that time, Ghana was known as the "Portuguese Gold Coast."

Next came the Dutch, who also began trading in the area and eventually secured strongholds from the Portuguese. The name changed to the "Dutch Gold Coast."* Under a set of treaties between the Netherlands and Great Britain, the English took control in 1872, changing the name yet again. In 1957, what had simply been known as the "Gold Coast" finally gained its independence after centuries of colony rule and subjugation. Ghana became the first sovereign Black country in Africa.

---

* One of Ghana's most important commodities has been gold. As a trading post (in commodities such as gold and cocoa but also, tragically, the transatlantic slave trade), it has experienced its share of piracy. Legend has it that a pirate who worked for a Dutch trading company often came to port under the darkness of night, quickly unloading and reloading cargo before anyone noticed. The locals of Elmina dubbed his ship the "night thief" and joked that this petite but muscular and clever smuggler was built for speed like the African wolf. Piracy, however, is not just a Hollywoodized story of adventure and mayhem. It can be terrifying in its reality. Piracy off the coast of Ghana remains present today.

This was, in part, thanks to the efforts and organizing of Kwame Nkrumah, a Ghanaian revolutionary, philosopher, and politician who served as the country's first prime minister and then president. Though many Americans might not know the history of Ghana and its peoples, aspects of this transitional period have been reimagined in popular culture — including the recent miniseries *The Crown*. Focusing on events from 1961, a season two episode depicts a meeting between Nkrumah and Queen Elizabeth II, when she traveled to Ghana to discuss the new country's young independence and its ideological ties to socialism. At a farewell ball, the two shared a dance. News photographs of the event — a White woman dancing with a Black man — shocked the sensibilities of some around the globe,[†] although this wasn't the first time Nkrumah had danced with English royalty.[‡] Meanwhile, across the pond, the Civil Rights Movement was transforming social norms, even as many places and practices in the United States remained highly segregated.

In the late nineteenth century, while still under British rule, Ghana also became the second largest producer of co-

---

[†] Ghana's history and culture are not often depicted in Western popular culture, nor always accurately. Journalist Tim McDonnell notes how the Netflix series *The Crown* fictionalized many of the historical details about this encounter and the country's leadership. Tim McDonnell, "*The Crown* Says One Dance Changed History: The Truth Isn't So Simple," NPR, January 21, 2018.

[‡] Several years earlier, Nkrumah danced with the Duchess of Kent at another royal ball.

coa in the world, another fact about this place my family and I did not know.

When the AFS letter arrived that Saturday in 1975, we were still very naïve about Ghana as well as other countries that share our globe. We had all kinds of questions: about the people, what they ate, what they thought of or knew about Americans. I was a blank slate, looking and ready for experiences to fill it.

New York

AFS had mailed me step-by-step instructions on how to get from LaGuardia Airport and into a transport that would take me to the Hotel Commodore. With a heavy backpack slung over my shoulders, I struggled to carry my suitcase as I maneuvered through the crowds. It was a cumbersome walk, but I was so excited that this did not phase me.

My adventure entailed many firsts: the first time on an airplane, the first time in New York, the first time encountering someone homeless and living on the street. It was also my first time staying in a hotel, eating hash browns, and (to the horror of a true Southerner!) drinking unsweetened iced tea.

The famous Hotel Commodore resembled something out of an old movie. A passageway from Grand Central Station guided me to its doors, and I entered the largest building I had ever seen, with walls that looked like they were made from solid stone. A huge staircase took me up to the lobby, and at the height of my climb, I saw banks of elevators and people bustling in all directions, seemingly lost in thought as they sought their destination. I was to share a room with another AFS recipient, an exchange student named Maria. We had so much space that we could have added two more girls! In 1975, Donald Trump and the Hyatt company offered to take it over and renovate it, and it reopened as the Grand Hyatt. Sadly, the hotel closed a year later, after which Donald Trump remodeled the hotel, stripping it of much of its original décor. I did not think it needed to be renovated. It was beautiful just the way I saw it.

We spent our time in New York at the AFS offices. There were twenty-one students in total; some would be staying in our host country for a full school year, while the rest of us would return after nine weeks. Upon seeing the diverse set of faces in the crowd, I could tell the selection team did a good job of scouting eager adventurers. We were encouraged to get to know one another and talk about our expectations and what we hoped to learn about ourselves. We also discussed what we hoped to give back to the people we were going to live with and meet. We then played some team-building games, designed to teach us how to communicate, be better listeners, build trust, and problem-solve, not just as individuals but together.

One game required teams of two. We took turns being both follower and leader, at first blindfolded and steered by the voice of the other, learning to listen for warnings about

New York

The Miriam and Ira D. Wallach Collection, The New York Public Library

Postcard of The Commodore Hotel, New York
Detroit Publishing Company (1913–1930)

obstacles and gaining trust in the care of someone else. The next day, we focused on the importance of leadership and connection. We built a structure that would fall when one piece was removed and came to appreciate the role each person plays in a group's success or failure. Another game asked us to link arms and form a tight circle — and then keep one student outside the circle from getting in. This game taught us what it is like to be excluded and shunned by the majority. We learned our lessons well. We were going to need them where we were going.

When it was time for the next leg on our journey, we traveled together by bus to Kennedy International Airport and then endured the lengthy process that begins most trips. We waited in line to check in, then surrendered our luggage for tagging and loading. Once done, we waited in another line to clear customs. Our passports and vaccination records were reviewed and validated. Only then were we ready to board, find our seats, and push back from the gate.

Across the pond we hopped!

It was a long hop: eleven hours. The travel time, however, gave us another opportunity to get to know each other a little more. When our excitement had died down, we found time to sleep. We stopped for fuel in Senegal, on the west coast of Africa, and were allowed to get off the plane and enter the airport. I made a trip to the bathroom first thing.

A woman, the bathroom attendant, stood outside the door handing out three squares of thin, brown tissue paper. I assumed it was the equivalent of toilet paper, though it looked different from what I was used to. The toilet, too, was so high off the floor that I had to work my short body to climb onto it. The flush tank was mounted on the wall above the commode, a chain dangling from it. I made another guess and pulled. Through a mix of gravity and motion, water filled the toilet bowl and cleared the area for the next customer.

After I washed my hands, the attendant perfumed the sinks to disguise any residual odor. There was an inconspicuous basket in an obvious location, so I tossed in some change — U.S. coins, which were all I had — and thanked her.

Many colorful booths dotted the interior of the airport itself. I thought the people were beautiful as well, their skin in rich shades of brown and wide, toothy smiles that gleamed in contrast. They were friendly and greeted me, perhaps hoping I would buy a souvenir. So many beautiful items danced in my eyes, but I was on a tight budget. I purchased some postcards to mail home sometime after I got settled. Then it was time to reboard.

Akwaaba Accra

We landed at the Kotoka International Airport in Accra at half past nine in the morning. We were two hours late in arriving, and it took another two hours to navigate customs.

As we disembarked, a luggage handler surprised me when he snatched my suitcase from my hands and carried it through the process. After I cleared customs, he asked me for a tip. I had thought the man was just being friendly! My cheeks flushed red, embarrassed that I did not know the custom. This wouldn't be the last time I embarrassed myself during my adventure. The good news was that I did not have to drag my own luggage. I was tired from the flight and the excitement. I perked up a bit when a customs officer asked me if I had brought a gun. My dumbstruck expression answered his question. He did not even open my bags. He merely smiled when I finally realized he was teasing.

AFS summer program, Ghana, 1975

"*Akwaaba!*" he said, which I learned is the Twi word for "welcome."

On the way to our youth hostel, the first thing I noticed was the abundance of lizards. They were at least twelve inches long and red and green in color. There were, of course, lizards in Georgia, tiny green ones about half the size of what I was now seeing. But I was beginning to notice the various similarities and differences as we traveled through this foreign land, the things I might have in common with the Ghanaian people and the gaps from which otherness would emerge. Skinks in Accra, chameleons back home—creatures that could change colors depending on where they were sitting and on what.

Everywhere, street vendors with little stands (or some with just crates) perched along the sides of the road. The women and children balanced baskets on top of their heads, wares hidden inside. It looked as if anything and everything could be found in this makeshift market. Radios, watches, and suitcases. Clothes and shoes. And food of endless variety: roasted corn on the cob, fresh pineapple, groundnuts, hard-boiled eggs, dried salted fish, shrimp, and some unknown meat on sticks.

Would I try one of these kabobs? What about the chickens that were clearly free-range? I would come to learn how the Ghanaians love eggs, a versatile source of protein. And delicious! (Just ask the countless creatures found throughout the animal kingdom who are ovivores...)

In downtown Accra, we stopped briefly at the local AFS headquarters on Kimberly Avenue for an impromptu meeting with the agency's volunteers. There was some confusion about where we would be staying for the next few days of orientation. There wasn't enough room for everyone in one place, so a few were placed in private homes and Maria and I volunteered to stay at a different youth hostel than the others. Our housemother was Mary.

She asked us to call her "Aunt Mary" and assured us that it was an all-female boardinghouse; she also did not approve of men coming there to visit. It was clean enough, and we were exhausted—grateful for any place to lie down. That is, until we discovered mice. One scurried across the floor in front of us. We screeched and squealed in stereotypical fashion and tried to climb onto something high.

After having a chance to rest, we returned to headquarters to regroup. Our trip was a part of AFS history because, in our cohort of students, there were six staying for a full school year. That had never been done before in Ghana. I, too, was a part of this history. Though I would be staying just a little more than two months, I was the first White female student assigned to central Ghana to live in a remote village.

Later that afternoon, we went to a restaurant called Ebony. It was not what we expected from a restaurant with such a sophisticated name. The floors seemed dirty, and cats roamed freely searching for scraps. Regardless, we had our first opportunity to sample Ghanaian food. Everyone was a little tentative, not sure just what it was we were eating, but we were all hungry and curious. The plates of white rice were topped with a spicy sauce the color of curry. Resembling the American version of stew, the dish was hot, flavorful, and surprisingly good — even if there were various ingredients that I could not readily name by taste or texture.

I thought about a Peace Corps volunteer we met on the airplane who shared an observation and some advice: In the first year in any new county, one might find a bug in a cup of coffee and then throw the whole cup of coffee out. In the second year, when such a hanger-on is discovered, it's usually plucked out. By the third year, one will hardly notice the visitor and simply drink the entire cup, coffee bug included! This insight would become key on many of my life's adventures. Simply being grateful to even have a cup of coffee.

We spent our week in Accra attending orientation sessions, taking language classes, participating in local events, and touring the area. It was a time to voice our apprehensions and expectations, similar to New York but now in a place where there was no going back. What did we hope to learn? What did we fear? What could we ever offer the people generously hosting us in their country and inviting us into their homes? There were basic safety lessons to attend to as well. We were cautioned about an illegal market in Accra, decades-long prison sentences or deportation if caught dealing drugs, and how we were vulnerable in certain places because of the color of our skin. This was an insight some of us might not have ever thought about before, something classmates and neighbors from different backgrounds back home understood all too well. Sure, we were American citizens with a U.S. embassy in Accra, but there were certain things AFS and even the embassy could not get involved with on our behalf. I had never heard of the term "black market" until we were cautioned to avoid anyone involved with it, and I did not know how I would recognize this even if I stumbled upon it. The term itself didn't sit well with me either.

On another morning at headquarters, we were offered lessons on etiquette. Whenever visiting another culture, it's all too easy to unintentionally offend someone. We were never to use our left hand in any type of interaction, not for greeting other people, pointing something out, eating, or giving or receiving items. In Ghanaian culture, one's left hand is for utilitarian things, and it's often considered the "toilet hand" for a reason. We also learned that a thumbs-up gesture, followed by a thumbs-down, is a swear word and should never be used.

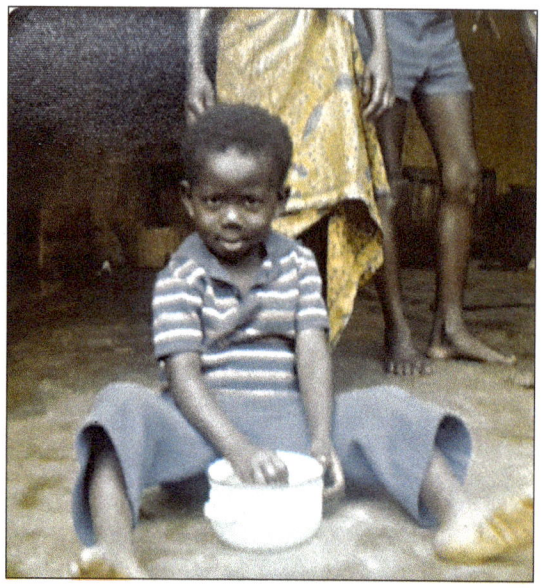

Kofi eating fufu

On the other hand, when we traveled around town, we had to become accustomed to individuals bathing on the sidewalks in between the local vendors organizing and selling their wares. The bathers took no notice of us, but I wasn't used to seeing folks naked, especially in public.

During afternoon breaks, we would go outside to wander the bustling street, purchase food from the local vendors, and play with the Ghanaian children who were as interested in us as we were about them. Some of the children wore Western clothing, but most had on traditional, vibrant sarongs — sometimes over a dress or a pair of slacks. Little boys tended to wear shorts with a T-shirt, the girls in simple dresses, shoes and sandals optional. One showed us how she used her colorful cotton cloth to wrap herself up at night and how she would lie down to sleep with it on. We tried to engage in conversations. With another little girl, I pointed to my chest and said my name: "Josie." She pointed to her chest and said, "*Chi chi*"—which meant "chest" in her native language. Somewhere in the world might still be a woman who thinks the English word for one's chest is "Josie." Oh, the funny connections and communions...and miscommunications!

After the incident with the mouse, Maria and I were rehoused with the Evans family. Mr. Evans was a prominent surgeon, and his wife was originally from Florida. They had three sons, Emmanuel Jr., Boozer, and Charlie, and one daughter named Rachel.

As we drove through the gate and into the family's compound, we noticed a sentry standing guard. Boozer explained to us that the family employed watchmen to protect against thieves. They had never had an intruder, but perhaps this was because of the extra security. Boozer said that, because guns were too noisy, the guards protected the family by bow and arrow—with arrows topped with poisoned tips. I couldn't tell if he was teasing.

The room that Marie and I shared was beautiful. Mr. Evans had servants who took care of everything, and the food prepared in his home was delicious. During this second night in Ghana, I had an opportunity to take a bath (a real luxury!) and then collapsed alongside Maria into a double bed that was very comfortable. Jet lag, the time difference, and the stress of moving to a new country and culture, even if temporarily, were beginning to catch up with me.

Sometime near dawn, while in a deep sleep, I dreamed about the guards and potential intruders. Maria's leg bumped into mine, startling me awake. I jumped straight up and out of bed, too scared to scream. What a laughable moment! Me and my imagination.

In the morning, we were greeted by servants who asked for our dirty clothes to wash. Then, they prepared breakfast and served it to us (another first for me): an egg omelet, fresh bread, fresh fruit, and coffee. My family had never had a cook or housekeeper, and I did not know how to respond. I tried to do the things that would have been expected of me at home, but one of Mr. Evans's servants would intervene and nudge me aside.

One night after dinner, Emmanuel Jr. and Boozer took us to a movie at the Orbit theater — a screened-in complex with ceiling fans and a movie screen showing five different films. We sat down in translucent plastic lawn chairs and were offered traditional popcorn and bottles of warm soda sipped through a straw. The boys opted for the local beer. The first movie was *The Three Musketeers*. In between films, there were commercials, including one about a spray promising to "squash a bug." Some of the other movies were foreign but dubbed in English or with subtitles. The last one we watched was a love story made in India. I drank my Coca-Cola — absent the ice that would have come with it back home — noticing that it tasted much sweeter. Like me, it had originated in Georgia yet found a home across an ocean in Ghana.

After the movie, we rode home in a taxi. The driver drove on the right side of the road, just like we did in the United States, but the car's steering wheel was positioned on the right side as well. I knew that the custom in England was to drive on the left, and it seemed that this taxicab would have been a better fit there. When I shared my thoughts about this curiosity, our driver explained that Ghana's driving directions had changed the year before. I imagined how much of an adjustment that must have been for everybody.

"Adjustment" would become the watchword for Maria and me and all the other members of our AFS cohort. There

Socializing with Ghanaian teenagers (Abena second from right)

was much to do and more to learn during orientation, and the remainder of the week was dizzying and dazzling.

How much would we grow and change — and "adjust" — after living with our host families? When would we get to meet them in person? We were anxious, in all senses of that word, for the "real" part of our journey but perhaps not quite ready.

We had met in New York, arrived in Accra, and dipped our toes in the shimmering pool of a new culture. But we were tadpoles still — tadpoles without legs! — and there was no telling how the coming experiences would shape just how high we'd learn to leap as the frogs we'd somehow become.

Long after orientation and after living with our host families, each of us would meet again in Accra, ever changed by our experiences. On one of these last nights in Ghana, a dance was held in our honor at the AFS headquarters, and we invited the children and others we had come to know to join us.

One of the little girls we had met that first week remembered me and ran down the hall to give me a hug. The fact that we were both hot and sticky did not matter.

Perhaps like some of the African children, I had never attended a dance where a disc jockey was in charge of the tunes, but the music he played was a mix of Ghanaian pop and American rock and roll. The boys from our group stood in a line to dance with the girls, and the girls waited for the boys to ask them to dance. We also did our best to socialize and dance with everyone who was willing. The Ghanaian girls kept telling us how beautiful we were, but perhaps they thought this because we were different. Different, yet the same, in so many ways. I thought they were beautiful too.

That evening, a little boy approached me and asked if he could travel with me when I went back home. I told him that my bag already exceeded the airline's allotted weight and there would be no way I could fit him in, but I knew that America was a dream for many people in Africa.

He had such a beautiful face and an even lovelier spirit.

Shirley

Who knew that becoming an exchange student would mean that I would get to meet Shirley? I decided to wear the pink dress that my grandmother had made.

During our first week in Ghana, in between the lessons and events and simply trying to adjust to a new culture, we were invited to the American embassy in Accra where we met Shirley.

As in Shirley Temple Black... the Shirley Temple who, as a young star in Hollywood, sang "On the Good Ship Lollipop." This child actress grew up to become a diplomat, eventually serving as chief of protocol for the United States, a delegate to the United Nations, and ambassador to Ghana and Czechoslovakia. President Gerald Ford had appointed her to the African assignment about seven months prior to our arrival.

Her foray into international politics began, so the story goes, in the late 1960s after Henry Kissinger bumped into her at a party. She was talking with others about Namibia, an African country struggling to gain its independence, and the (apparently) startling contrast of this American star speaking eloquently about African history and governance upended Kissinger's preconceived notions about her talents. As she once stated, he was "surprised that I even knew the word" or anything else about Namibia. She was not just that curly-haired cutie Kissinger remembered from his youth.[*]

The Ghanaians called her "Shirley" as a sign of affection and respect.

It was strange standing next to this celebrity whom I knew from watching her movies. She was about my height and size and three decades older than me, but perhaps like Kissinger, in my mind she was still that dimpled little girl with wide eyes, precocious smile, and golden ringlets framing her face. I could see a trace of that iconic Shirley when she greeted us at the embassy, especially as her expressions changed from delighted to serious and then back to delighted again.

She brought us into her office for a group photo. We circled around her as she settled into her chair, gracefully crossing her legs. We arranged ourselves with Shirley front and center. She asked about each of us and where we were from, then tended to us like a mother hen: telling us to keep a close

---

[*] Joshua Keating, "Shirley Temple Black's Unlikely Diplomatic Career," *Slate*, February 11, 2014.

National Portrait Gallery (E.M. Warnecke)

Portrait of Shirley Temple by Harry Warnecke and Lee Elkins (1938)

eye on our money, warning us about the illegal market and the dangers of drugs, reminding us to take our antimalaria pills and not to drink the local water. And lastly, of course, to have a good time. We promised to return at the end of our adventures to share our experiences with her.

And indeed, we did see Shirley again, after the adventures that would come in between this first meeting and heading home. For our second encounter, Shirley invited us to visit the embassy residence, located in a neighborhood with ambassadors from other embassies. The house was tastefully decorated with memorabilia from Shirley's childhood. Family photos precious to her were positioned around the room. We gazed in awe but were also excited to share with Shirley our adventures.

After lunch, we gathered around her feet, and she asked us questions about our experiences. A cacophony erupted in the room — we all wanted to speak at once! She laughed and marveled with us as we discussed the details of our awkward blunders and other mishaps as well as our many discoveries. It was a great capstone to the entire exchange student experience.

Or as one might say...sharing this with Shirley was sweeter than any "trip to a candy shop / Where bonbons play / On the sunny beach of Peppermint Bay."

SHIRLEY

The students of the AFS summer program with Ambassador Shirley Temple Black at her embassy residence in Ghana

Elmina Castle

Orientation wasn't all fun and games.

Yet visiting Elmina Castle was one of the most important day trips we took at the beginning of our exchange student journey. Despite having grown up in the South, I did not know much about the transatlantic slave trade as a seventeen-year-old in 1975 (two years before the miniseries *Roots* would open the eyes of large swaths of the American public), and I could not fully grasp the significance of such a sacred historical place.

In the village of Elmina, a mix of modern buildings and shack-like housing—some with straw roofs, some with no roofs at all—greeted us. So did the town's street vendors, many of whom looked biracial.

Elmina Castle, located on the shores of the Gulf of Guinea, was built by the Portuguese and once known as

Oladapo Olusola

Elmina Castle, also known as St. George of the Mine Castle, in Ghana

Castelo de São Jorge da Mina. Its names reflect the long history of mining in the region, both before colonization and after. The castle, or fort, was first constructed as a trading post and is the oldest European structure in this part of Africa. When the trade in humans grew more valuable than the trade of gold, the fort expanded and became a center for detaining and processing slaves.

During the transatlantic slave trade, even as the fort changed hands from the Portuguese to the Dutch and then the British, tens of thousands of Africans passed through Elmina. Slave traders — and the industries, laws, and societies that supported them — subjugated fellow human beings to the horrors of bondage.

Western traders would arrive in Elmina, their ships laden with goods for trade or sale. On their return, their hulls became dungeons for individuals and families, kidnapped or captured in war and bartered away to places far beyond home.

The ships sailed across the Atlantic to South America, then eventually North America, and the islands off their coasts in between. By the early nineteenth century, approximately twelve million Africans had been enslaved.

Remnants of the transatlantic slave — whether in structures like Elmina and the racism and socioeconomic disparities that continue to linger today — are still visible in Ghana and beyond.

This was why the AFS made sure we visited Elmina Castle and, even in the quiet of our contemplation as we stood on that site, might begin to understand this deplorable part of human history.

I made notes at the time so that I would never forget:

> Individuals captured specifically to be enslaved and traded were brought to this castle that sits on the coastline of Ghana. Upon arrival, the men and women were separated, with the latter detained on a lower floor and the former on an upper floor. The conditions in which these humans were imprisoned were inhumane. Two rooms were earmarked for punishment. The first, called a "warning cell," was large with windows that were barred. The second was smaller and had

limited openings for air and sunlight. Those who were deemed "uncooperative" would be kept here, tortured and denied food and water for three days. If they were still alive on the third day, they were taken to the hillside and decapitated. When traders came to bargain, they were allowed to peruse the women through openings in the floor. As a courtesy, a woman would be provider to share their bed at night. If during the length of their stay the woman became pregnant, she was released to live outside the castle in the village of the same name.

Elmina Castle sat idle for many years until Ghana gained its independence. It was officially designated a World Heritage Monument in 1979.

Later, as I continued to learn more about this chapter in human history, I better recognized the connections between Elmina and other places in Africa and my own hometown. When the colonial settlement of Georgia was first established by Gen. James Oglethorpe in the 1730s, it was the only English colony that prohibited slavery. That prohibition did not last, however, particularly after Oglethorpe stepped back in his leadership roles and returned to England for good. Slavery then became institutionalized in Georgia as it had elsewhere in what would become the Southern United States.

The descendants of the slaves from the central and western regions of Africa brought to the Carolinas, Florida, and

Georgia are known as the Gullah Geechee, who continue to practice many of the traditions of their ancestors. With days of remembrance and festivals celebrating their rich cultures, they are colleagues, neighbors, and friends who help us all to remember the wondrous diversity of human life and the consequences of dehumanizing others. Perhaps we are making small steps, as when President Joe Biden made Juneteenth a federal holiday, but this history is a reminder that there larger and many more steps to go.

Kumasi to Sunyani

With orientation finally over, it was time to leave Accra and embark on the next stage of this journey — one that would split into many paths as each of us traveled in different directions to meet our host families.

We broke into smaller groups and left Accra by bus. Not in the charter buses that we had been taking on our various trips throughout the week, but Ghanaian transports. These weren't all that different, though, and they were very nice. In fact, we had gotten to know the bus station well during our time in Ghana's capital. It was like bus stations everywhere — with seats on which to rest while waiting, bathrooms of some sort, and a place to buy drinks, fruit, and other travel snacks. What bothered me about this bus station and the many places we visited in Ghana were the people trying to make a living by begging on the streets. This not only unnerved me but made my heart hurt. The same faces would be there every time we arrived, trying to gather enough coins to eat. Some were injured or lived with a disability. A good bit of my coins when into their cups.

After about six hours, the bus I had taken from Accra, along with four others from our group, finally pulled into Kumasi and stopped on an unpaved patch of dusty ground off the city's main traffic circle. There was no depot here. This was where all buses, taxis, and lorries picked up passengers and packages. It was late, and all we could see was what was visible in the cone of the headlights.

Our escort on the trek could only find us one room for the night. We had to decide how we were going to share the one bed. I was the only girl. One of the boys opted for the floor, but I wasn't too sure what crawly thing would find me there, so I petitioned for a sliver of the mattress that hopefully would keep me safe. We slept side by side, longways. We were so exhausted, we did not care about the uncomfortable position.

Early the next morning, we returned to the area we were dropped off the night before. Our group branched again: C.L. and I had to travel in a different direction from the others. He would be left in Sunyani with his host family, and I was to journey a little farther to Chiraa to meet the Boateng family.

We switched to a lorry, or a "mammy wagon" as the locals called them: converted flatbed trucks with added-on covers and wooden slats for seats strong enough to support luggage, local farm products, and people. The more the merrier was a popular opinion in Ghana. All types of farm ani-

Eggi

A "mammy wagon" in Ghana named for Psalm 23

mals and food products were stuffed in and around us and stacked as high as could be managed. The lorry drivers were a serious lot and always soliciting for weary travelers.

Each lorry was proudly christened with a traditional local saying, the name of someone world-famous, or a proverb from the Bible. Reading these always made me smile. There was the *Muhammad Ali*, the *Kennedy*, the *Queen Mother*, *Our Shepherd*, and *Heaven Bound*. Alongside the lorries, and really everywhere in Kumasi, there were people on foot and on bicycles, sometimes balancing cold box compartments proffering Fanta soda, juices, beer, and GoldenTree chocolate.

Kwaku Boateng, Abena's nephew, in traditional clothing

The lorries and taxis were always given the right-of-way, unless a group of farm animals was crossing the road.

Over the coming weeks, I would revisit Kumasi many times. It was the transportation hub in this region of Ghana — the conduit that connected me to anywhere I needed to go — as well as the home of the Kumasi Zoo, a favorite pastime of mine.

As our lorry chugged on and the day lengthened, I spent time studying the surroundings. The ground was red clay, like the red clay in Georgia and Alabama. In between orange-colored villages that blurred together as we passed, greenery would peek out.

The modest homes and rough huts in the villages (as I would later better understand) often served as both residence and shop, at least for those who could afford such an arrangement. Others would gather to sell products and merchandise in a communal market area that each village had. Sometimes a vendor would simply place pieces of clothing or other items on the ground, all neatly displayed.

When we arrived in Sunyani, C.L.'s host brother, Henry Opoku Ware, greeted us as we stepped from the lorry. There was no time to look around as my next transport was leaving shortly. I said goodbye to C.L. and tried to hide my sadness and apprehension as we parted. I wouldn't know anyone as I traveled to Chiraa; every face would be new, smiling or not. C.L. and I promised to meet each other often. After all, we were only twelve miles apart, right?

In Ghana, twelve miles is a long way.

Chiraa

At long last, the village of Chiraa, once but a fantasy in my imagination, came into focus as we neared. Somewhere here lived Agnes Boateng, my host sister, along with her extended family. Chiraa looked like many of the villages I had seen on my long trek: structures in various shades of orange or built from combinations of handmade cement blocks and red clay. Acacia trees, large enough to provide much-needed shade, grew in the gaps in between homes and stores. Under the acacias, folks gathered to talk, play games, or wait for transportation. In 1975, the village was so small that the Boatengs' box at the post office was number six as was the telephone number of the eldest brother of the family, who had one of the few phones in Chiraa.

When my host sister and I finally met face-to-face, her wide smile was shy but welcoming and matched my own. Agnes and I chatted, while her eleven-year-old brother,

Richard, retrieved my bags and carried them as we walked. We talked hesitantly at first, but then our conversation flowed fast as new friends, and a part of me couldn't believe I was actually here. She also explained why her family called her "Abena." Navigating the streets of Chiraa, we eventually arrived at the Boateng compound, a large square of land with multiple structures.

Abena's house faced the main road leading into the village, though it was set back far enough and surrounded by trees that it radiated a hospitable feeling. Other homes were next to and behind this house, each topped by a tin roof that made a comforting sound when it rained. Together, they formed an inner courtyard that provided privacy from the neighbors and a place for the family to gather. This plaza was the heartbeat of the family home — where children played as the women cooked, and the radio chirped from sunup to sundown. Journalists from the BBC would compete with the roosters to crow about the first news of the day. In the afternoons, popular African tunes interspersed with the top one hundred from the United States. "Black Superman," a Johnny Wakelin song about Muhammad Ali — the "king of the ring" who "floats like a butterfly and stings like a bee" — played every hour throughout the summer. Courtyard congregations grew larger when friends stopped by to socialize or parties or funerals were held. The entire village was built in variations on this traditional style, except for the priest's home and the Catholic church.

Abena ushered me into her house and gave me a quick tour. There was an alcove near the back that served as a food

Richard (far right) and others talking to Akosua

prep kitchen and a bathroom in the rear left corner. A small, pantrylike storeroom held limited supplies because most food and other items—like the coal needed to fuel the hibachi stoves—were bought daily from the local open-air market. When it was time to cook, a child would be assigned to squat next to the brazier and fan the flames with a device made of straw. Anything cold was kept in a small refrigerator at the eldest brother's house, the repository for the family's more modern equipment. Daily, the women would pre-

Abena's father in traditional clothing

pare fufu — often requiring three of them to establish a solid rhythm to pound the boiled yam roots into pulp. If they missed a beat, someone's hand was liable to get caught in the mix.

The bathroom was both similar and different to what I used at home. It was a simple room, about six feet square, with a drain hole in the center. When someone needed to bathe, one of the children in the family would fetch a bucket of water and heat it on a makeshift burner in the kitchen area. It was a process I struggled to figure out. Should I wash my hair first and then work my way down or vice versa? The solution was two buckets of warm water. I also asked for a nail to be hammered into the door, from which to hang my stuff. Then I mentioned how nice it would be to have something to sit on or a place to rest my foot on while washing. Soon, a rubber battery cover showed up in the room. Once done, I would empty the bucket in the direction of the drain (which I suspected also was used as a quick urinal), and the sun quickly evaporated the dirty water.

The rest of the house consisted of several eight-by-ten-foot rooms, each with at least one shuttered window that looked onto the courtyard. The windows were opened early every morning and closed before bed. No glass. No screens. Just open air.

One double room was reserved for Abena's father, who managed his cocoa farm, Bredi, and was not present when I first arrived. In the center was a large, hand-carved bed made from native wood. When he wasn't home, the door was kept locked, and only Abena's mother had the key. Everyone else slept in another assigned room, some with beds, some with bedrolls, or a space in the courtyard.

Abena and I were to share her room, painted a pale orange. I was given her one small bed, while she rolled out a pallet each night. She said she preferred sleeping this way, and I would soon learn that she often was restless at night and would wake at odd hours. It reminded me of the time that I startled Maria with my Evans family dreams. I was grateful for Abena's hospitality, and the arrangement worked for us

Akosua Broni with some members of Abena's family in Chiraa

both. We would spend many a good hour in this room, especially when female friends visited after the younger children went to bed.

Other rooms in the house were painted a bright blue. At the time, I didn't think much of it, nor did Abena have any explanation as to why. Perhaps her family simply liked the color? Later I would learn, far from Chiraa and while touring a historic building in Savannah, that this may have been "haint" blue, a color derived from indigo plants that the Gullah Geechee use to protect their homes and confuse evils spirits into thinking this is water or the sky.

More recently, Abena and I reminisced about my first time in her house and how much we still share in common:

"My granddaughters visited me over the weekend," Abena told me. "The youngest child, who has just learned how to bathe, noticed a bucket in the shower of my bathroom. 'Grandma, show me how to use the bucket,' she said. So I did. Later, she reported: 'It is better than using the shower, because it frees both hands, and you don't need a shower cap. You can also control the use of your water. Showers are all over the place.'"

My mother's mother took care of me until I was about six. We had indoor plumbing, but at the time it was new — installed not long before I arrived into the world. In our house, there was a bathroom next to the kitchen. It consisted of a claw-foot tub, a toilet, a sink, a mirror, and a handmade shelf. My older cousins used to put their chewing gum under the shelf. Being little, I looked up at it every time I sat down.

My grandmother did not like to take baths because, as a small child, she almost drowned. She used a steel bucket that she kept inside the tub. Hot water, soap, and a washcloth. She bathed me the same way. After soaping me all over, she gently rinsed me with cups of warm water. Very soothing... and similar experiences. A process taught to me by my grandmother.

Fufu: The Mother Dish

My first morning in Chiraa, I woke up to roosters crowing in the distance and the sound of somebody sweeping the courtyard. I could hear lyrical voices shouting out morning greetings, in between talking and laughter. The radio blared the morning news, though later the earworm "Kung Fu Fighting" would take its place.

One of Abena's younger sisters brought me my breakfast on a tray. Steam from a delicious cup of MILO cocoa reached my nose, as did the smell of the bread baked daily in a stone oven. There was also fruit and scrambled eggs. I ate in Abena's room, isolated from the others, because this was the way they served their guests. After breakfast, Abena rejoined me and stood at the window to fix her hair. She loved singing, and this morning, her beautiful voice lilted a rendition of Tom Springfield's "I'll Never Find Another You," made popular a decade earlier by The Seekers.

We then joined other members of the Boateng family in the courtyard. Everyone appeared busy, concentrating on their tasks. Little girls — Abena's younger sisters and nieces, perhaps with neighborhood friends in the mix — played version of jacks. Instead of bouncing a small ball before quickly scooping up metal jacks, they used pebbles: tossing one pebble into the air and collecting the other pebbles before the first hit the ground. A few boys, including Richard and other relatives, kicked a ball around. It wasn't always a ball they used on these occasions; other items would stand in when a ball couldn't be found.

The women of Abena's family, and some of the older girls, were busy in the outdoor kitchen area, and we went over to watch and help. They were making fufu — a signature Ghanaian food that is a staple across many communities (even if different populations sometimes spell and pronounce the word differently). What were the staples where I grew up? I wasn't sure, perhaps white bread and rice. Fufu contained far better ingredients to meet the nutritional needs of the population.

Preparing the dish, however, was no easy task. Abena's mother, Akua Manu, alongside other kin and neighbors, perched on stools, first washing and then peeling yams — though sometimes the dish is made with other root vegetables like cassava and cocoyam or even plantains. The yams are then boiled in a pot until they reach the right tenderness. I had seen similar preparations in my grandmother's kitchen with potatoes, corn on the cob, turnip greens, and the like. My grandmother might have shucked corn on the back porch, but this outdoor assembly line was a whole new level of food prep for me.

Mashing came next. Requiring strength, trust, and patience — and a coordinated team effort — perhaps it was no wonder the women were in charge. The yams, now boiled and ready, were placed in large, hand-carved wooden bowl similar to a mortar and pestle. One woman was assigned to the "pounding pole," the *woma*, as Abena explained. The name for the bowl was *waduro*.

Together, these two implements, much like the three women who began to mash in symphonic unison, are essential to the art form of fufu. The wood of the bowl must be strong enough not to crack under the pressure, or shards will mix in with the rest of the ingredients. The *woma* as well can't be flimsy, and it must be nonporous and smooth. Perhaps like a butter churn — though more laborious.

I watched as Abena's relatives coordinated their timing, thinking of the moments I would help my grandmother mash potatoes or other ingredients using a handheld tool that would someday become my own, as this particular *woma* would become Abena's. The women developed a rhythm, trusting one another and listening to the sounds, adding water when appropriate and keeping fingers clear. The music of fufu-making filled the air. I became mesmerized.

I wanted to help and was eager to try. Abena's mother handed me the *woma*, but my efforts merely produced stifled giggles from some of the others and comments in Twi. Though I didn't understand their exact words, I agreed with their thoughts: I likely would do more harm than good, and it was better I stay a spectator. The next step — forming the mashed ingredients into soft balls — was more my speed.

In another area of the plaza, other women prepared the flavorful soup that goes with the dough. Depending on the availability of ingredients, this could be a broth made from palm nuts or groundnuts and include fresh tomatoes, onions, and chilis. One of the women gave me a taste — an explosion of flavors like none I had ever had. Ginger, paprika, peppers. Delicious...and spicy enough to make my nose run.

Enough fufu is made to last the entire day, so that individuals can ladle a portion whenever they grow hungry. But it must be made daily, or it spoils. Mornings are for fufu-making, and it's typically ready by noon. Bread, corn, and fruit supplement the daily fare.

The final product done, everyone was proud and eager for me to try it. Abena's mother portioned some of the broth into smaller serving bowls, the size that would feed four individual people eating soup back home, and we situated ourselves around the vessels. Abena showed me how to pinch off a bit of fufu — with my right hand only! — and use it to sop up the soup, swallowing both together. But I struggled with this. I simply could not get a small enough piece of fufu lubricated with a big enough portion of broth to make them slide down my throat without choking. (A similar situation happened the first time I tried oysters at home.) I could see in my hosts' eyes that they were disappointed I couldn't fully enjoy the experience. With kindness and love, they began making my fufu with rice (perhaps this was my staple food!).

Regardless, never a drop was wasted: If it dripped off your hand and ran to your elbow, it was natural to rescue this treat with your tongue. No one thought less of you.

The fufu was even fancier on Sundays — with an added mixture of meat, chicken, and fish. Sunday dinners in Ghana reminded me of Sunday dinners at home. With my family in the United States, we would eat roast beef or chicken and vegetables, plus a dessert reserved for Sundays and special occasions. Whoever cooked (usually my mom or grandmother) prepared the main dishes alone, though others helped with the rest of the meal. Perhaps not as coordinated of an effort as my new Ghanaian family, but something much the same. As different as different cultures and dishes can be throughout this diverse world, ingredients and seasonings share commonalities. Sitting around a table with loved ones is universal fare.

As Ghanaians like to say, the "fufu has fallen into the soup."

Despite being a picky eater, I had fallen as well.

Father and Family

Abena's father sent several cocoyams ahead of his arrival. They were to celebrate my stay with the family, and when he came home, it was quite ceremonial. Seated in the courtyard on an Ashanti stool, he was dressed in the finest Ghanaian kente cloth.

He was tall, even sitting down, and he reminded me of Mr. Clean and Yul Brynner in *The King and I*. When he rose, he walked with his hands clasped behind his back, with perfect posture and both pride and grace. He looked slightly to the left and then to the right to survey his surroundings. A tiny sound of approval could be detected when I listened close enough.

As we were formally introduced, he reached out his hand and smiled. His whole face brightened. I felt welcomed and honored as he regarded me with kind eyes. I also would come to know and appreciate his great sense of humor.

Pernilla Klockars

Cocoa beans from Ghana

I had brought several gifts with me from the States, as my AFS guides had encouraged. I wanted to bring a little bit of Georgia to Ghana, including a tin of pecans. I also had been involved with selling Avon cosmetics when I was sixteen, and I had quite a bit of unopened samples. I presented the patriarch of the Boateng family with ten tiny bottles of women's perfume that he could give to his wives as he saw fit. He opened the bottles one by one, smelling the aromas, and then decided he would keep them for himself!

Abena's father had four wives over the course of his life but only two when I came to stay with the family. One wife had left after a divorce, another had passed away. Abena's mother stayed in Chiraa on home duty, as the other wife took her turn working with their husband on the cocoa farm. Once or twice a year, the two wives would alternate. There was no such thing as "your" children and "my" children. It was "our" children who comprised the family. Older siblings took care of younger siblings, and it was not unusual to see the former "wearing their siblings" on their backs while they worked and played.

This was the way small children were transported from place to place: tucked securely into a long piece of fabric wrapped around the caregiver's waist. I had never seen babies carried like this before, but it was smart and done in such a way that a knot or an expert fold prevented the child from slipping out. It freed up one's hands to do other things — work or play, make crafts or shop. Of course, I had to try it. I wished I had known about this when I was pulling my siblings around by hand.

Senior Brother, Oppong "Benjamin" Boateng, was the eldest son of the family, and his mother was the wife who had passed away. He also had four wives and lived in the house behind Abena's — complete with a black-and-white television set converted to color by a piece of colored plastic placed over the screen. I remember walking into the house one evening when a crowd had gathered to watch *Starsky and Hutch*. I was asked if we all drove in cars like the one on TV. "No," I said, "only those two guys do." Senior Brother drove a Mercedes-Benz. He kept it in a clay-built garage that had attached to it the only outhouse in town.

One day, I visited Senior Brother's place of work. It was located halfway between Chiraa and Sunyani. He had studied medicine in England and had returned home to practice. His clinic did not look like any doctor's office I had ever visited. It was decorated with lit candles and statues of Jesus and Mary — along with what looked to be amulets and charms. He seemed to practice a mix of modern medicine, homeopathic medicine, and traditional medicine, with a little Catholic and West African juju as part of the healing.

He told me as much. He used his knowledge of modern medicine and applied homeopathic remedies to treat the patients who came to see him. He also said he could call on spirits to help him heal the people who were sick, bodily and spiritually. I wandered into one of the rooms that must have been his pharmacy. Shelves filled with small jars and bottles displayed labels that read "to get pregnant," "to prevent heart trouble," "to treat constipation," and the like. He cared for the people from his village and others using a mix of modern and alternative medicine to complement his cures, as such practices were coming back into vogue in the United States.

My adopted teen siblings also decided that I was a dud when it came to washing my clothes. They snickered at my efforts, but it was my first experience cleaning clothes by hand. Back home, we had a washing machine. It was almost as old as me, and I don't remember a day when clothes were washed any other way.

So, the younger sisters would gather my clothes and clean them using three buckets: one to wet the dirty duds, one with soap to wash the pieces by hand, and one to rinse. Like making fufu, this required physical strength. I wanted to help, and I tried — but they would lose themselves in giggles and shoo me away. At least I could assist once my clothes emerged from bucket number three. We draped the clean garments (including my underwear) over the courtyard banisters to dry in the sun. The girls then used a cast-iron, coal-heated iron to press my clothes. I still owe them a tip.

Richard also snuck into my heart, a very adventurous child forever etched in my thoughts and life. He spoke British English very well and, ever patient, helped me to understand the customs and differences in language. His daily job involved walking to a small stream on the other side of the village to fetch fresh water. Others gathered there throughout the day to do the same for their families. Richard would carry a large water bucket at his side on the way there. Once filled, he would lift it onto his head — the water sloshing over the edges as he carefully navigated back home. By the time he arrived, he'd be drenched! Maneuvering the bucket with his strong shoulders and back (such a task makes one sturdy, even at age eleven), Richard would pour the remaining water into a barrel and top this with a lid. This cistern provided water for cleaning, bathing, and cooking, boiled first before being used for the latter two.

Richard also was skillful in making soap[*] and procuring rubber. He once went into the jungle where he knew rub-

---

[*] And, as an adult, he moved to Belgium to work for a company that produces detergent.

Oliver Schmid

Rubber tapping

ber trees grew —*funtumia elastica*, the scientific name of this African tree and so very apt for a boy who always engendered fun.

Using his favorite knife and some buckets, he cut the tree's trunk into small, angled slices so that the latex would seep out and flow directly into each pail that he rigged lower on the tree. The average time to tap a gallon of sap is about six hours, and I saw him coming and going throughout the day, walking with purpose. By late afternoon, he returned with a container of sticky liquid. I watched him pour it out on a smooth cement surface in a shaded area of the courtyard.

The next day, when he decided it was ready, he sliced the rubber into long strips — carefully cutting different lengths and widths. To create a bouncy ball, he rolled a small, palm size amount in his hands until it became smooth and round. He tested his product by bouncing it until he was satisfied with the way it performed. Other strips were used to make the skin for drums and, somehow (I don't know how he managed it), others were turned into soccer balls. I knew then that I had to find room in my suitcase for one of Richard's wonders. It was fascinating.

I often think of Richard in the same vein as another boy from Ghana who loved science and taking things apart to see how they worked. Ave Kludze Jr. grew up in Accra and fell in love with aviation when he visited Kotoka International Airport with his father. After his initial schooling, he immigrated to the United States to study electrical engineering and systems engineering, eventually earning his doctorate and then going to work for NASA. He became the first Ghanaian astronaut to fly a spacecraft! Two curious, creative boys, both from humble beginnings. From drying latex in a courtyard to flying in space. What a bounce!

Girl Talk

When we were home in the evenings, we would sit around and talk, or I'd play with the local children who stopped by to see me, this White girl from America. They and my siblings had a lot of questions for "Akosua Broni." She also had quite a few of her own.

The children would call out for me to meet them outside, and I often had to think of something to do to keep everyone entertained. It started with just a few at first, but by the time I was set to leave Ghana, more than two hundred kids would arrive. Older, younger, and all ages in between. We played games — like duck, duck, goose; red light, green light; and "Mother May I?" — and I taught them the "Hokey Pokey" and "We're Going to Kentucky (We're Going to the Fair)." They taught me games too. We danced and shared songs, some familiar to us both. Their favorite to sing to me was about a White woman born on a Sunday whose moth-

Chiraa children playing duck, duck, goose with Akosua Broni

er made rice water: *Abrewa ei pam noo, Akosua Broni neekoro no* ("Old lady, run after her, there goes the Sunday-born White girl")...*Akosua Broni maame ei rice water, ei ei rice water.*

We often would end our time with a rendition of "Jesus Loves Me." The words were different than how I learned them, but the melody was the same, further proving to me how God is multilingual. Eventually, their parents and other villagers would gather round to watch and laugh. As darkness set in, Abena would retrieve me so the children could go home.

One day, I taught some of the younger Boateng family members how to make paper hats using newspaper. I also outlined figures on blank paper, and we cut out paper dolls. We made clothes for them with scraps of fabric. Sometimes, the girls would practice braiding my hair. It was hard work because my own brunette locks were so fine compared to theirs.

After the younger siblings went to bed (and the village children returned to their respective homes), Abena's room would fill up with older female relatives and friends. It was time for "girl talk," and everyone would sit, lay down, or lounge wherever a spot could be found. We asked each other questions and made comparisons between life in the United States versus Ghana.

The first topic of conversation I could not resist raising was the practice of polygyny. I had heard about it in the Bible and in relation to the Mormon faith, but I had never seen it practiced. I was raised Catholic. What I knew in my (very insular) seventeen years of life was one husband–one wife, whether the wedding was held in a courtroom or a church. In Ghana, a man could marry as many wives and have as many children as he could afford. The more children, the more help on a family farm or in the family business.

"How does all this work?" I wanted to know.

A friend of Abena's explained, "When it is time to marry, a man selects you. He starts visiting more frequently and giving gifts. If the woman accepts the gifts, she is consenting to the courtship. Three dates are common. The man then visits your father to ask for permission to marry you. The father, and sometimes the mother, will consider the man's background, financial stability, and social status."

"And then, if permission is granted," Abena took up the story from there, "the woman goes to the man's home to spend the night. If he is happy with the evening, they get married."

That is what my companions told me, but still fascinated with the concept, I later searched for more information. Sometimes, it seemed, gifts were not given, nor did every couple become intimate before marriage, especially if a courtship started in church. In other settings, women remained very independent: living separately from the men with whom they had relationships and not always knowing exactly who had fathered which child.

"In America," I described, as Abena was braiding my hair and having somewhat better luck than the younger girls, "a girl might have a boyfriend or the prospect of a boyfriend. They might flirt with each other or express their interest through teasing and banter. Or make out!" They asked me what this meant. They had other names for the activity.

The courting practice of gift-giving might have explained why young men often brought me presents when they visited the family.

One of the neighbors, whom Abena called "Superman," called on me more than once. He already had seven wives! Still, he offered to marry me and said that he would divorce his other wives if I agreed.

"I'm only seventeen!" I told him, though that seemed old enough to him and did not dissuade him. "I'm still in school. I can't marry you or anyone else now." He retreated in dismay.

In a given family, there was a pecking order among the wives. The newest wife handled the lowest housekeeping tasks. Among Senior Brother's spouses, one such job was cleaning the outhouse attached to the garage. We were blessed in the Boateng family to have this privy and the luxury of toilet paper provided just for me. The younger siblings often would "escort" me. One would lead the group with my roll of toilet paper perfectly balanced on her head, and they all would mill around until I came out. At night, it was trickier because I would have to light a lantern; more accurately, I would have to wake Abena to light the lantern before making the rest of the way on my own. And, as I quickly learned, it was essential to use the roughly made whisk to swat at the flies so I could sit down without surprises.

Other families were relegated to the public latrine, a cement block building a short distance from their houses. One side was for males, the other for females, with basic drainage holes in the floors. Livestock and children often wandered in and out. The cocoa farm had a six-by-six-foot pit toilet with wooden slates across the gap. It was down a path, and before arriving, it was customary to shout "*Algo*!" in case someone was already there. I was fearful when trying to straddle the slats — afraid of missing one and falling in. I quickly found a private place in the jungle for such "necessities." I kept a watchful eye for the curious critters who could surprise me.

Wives sometimes were tasked with selling items in the marketplace or working as a teacher or hairdresser. And childcare was everyone's responsibility, older siblings included.

In Ghana and other African societies, there are traditions and ceremonies to celebrate the various stages of life as well as death — with some rituals resembling those of other cultures around the world and some that are very different. One tradition in Abena's community was to mark the cheeks of newborns. This was done by cutting a small gash in a baby's cheek and filling it with potash and special herbs to create a raised scar when it healed. Abena and all of her kin bore the mark.

The mark holds layers of significance. First, it is spiritual, representing a historic moment in an individual's life. By "flawing" the skin, it also provides protection against the spirits of the underworld, who are always on the lookout for "perfect" babies. In an era and area where not all infants survived, the scars are lifelong reminders that a child escaped this near-death experience. Second, it is tribal, as each community marks the face differently: One's lineage becomes identifiable in peacetime or war (when it may be difficult to tell friend from foe). And, finally, it is ornamental, similar to the American version of a beauty mark or a tattoo.

At one point, I was offered the ceremony. Honored to be asked, I almost agreed, until Abena explained the procedure and I thought about how this might play out back home.

Shortly after birth, girls also have their ears pierced and are given their first string of hip beads. My ears were already pierced — one trait I shared with my new sisters and friends. I graciously and enthusiastically accepted my own hip beads. As children develop, each set of hip beads is exchanged for better fitting ones, which creates a growing collection.

The beads serve multiple purposes as a rite of passage and symbol of femininity: to help the hips mature as a girl becomes a woman, to manage one's weight, to attract Ghanaian men. The more hip beads a woman wore, the greater the sound when she walked and danced, the more alluring to potential suitors. Already a teenager, my hips were more that of woman than child, and I accepted every gift of hip beads offered. Since I traveled so much on foot and was still learning to eat Ghanaian food, I didn't need help with weight control.

Hip beads have another use.

One day, I watched as Abena gathered strips of cotton. I asked her what she was doing, and she said she was preparing for her "menstrual."

"You mean your period?" I asked.

At the time, this was how Ghanaian women managed the monthly occurrence. Thin strips of cotton were fashioned into a pad, kept in place with a strand of cotton secured to the front and back of their hip beads.

My first experiences were similar: When it was time, my mother introduced me to a blue box with a white rose on it and the concept of a "feminine napkin." It was the most uncomfortable thing to have to wear during my time of the month, but it worked in a comparable fashion. This also was attached to the front and back of one's undercarriage—though by an elastic belt with two metal clips that caught the ends of the strand after you pulled it through. By the time I traveled to Chiraa, my knowledge and practice included self-adhering pads and tampons. I stockpiled both for my trip to Ghana and shared them with Abena. The supply was left with her when I went home. From time to time, she would write and ask that I send her more.

Hip beads were one of the main souvenirs I brought back to the United States. I wore at least a dozen on my hips on the plane, and they made lovely gifts for my girlfriends and family. Nowadays, women wear them under their clothing, when they go to the beach, even for photo shoots. Such stylish hip jewelry is a nice way to honor ourselves as women, and I always tried to remember the many different meanings.

These evenings in Abena's room — where female friends and relatives could let their hair down (or braid it up!) from their many responsibilities — were filled with fellowship and laughter. Just like at home.

Some stories were funny, some thought-provoking or sad. Often both.

One was about a monkey who had lost one of her babies. She would visit Chiraa from time to time. That did not bother anyone, until the monkey started taking infants from the village. The children were always found somewhere, usually safe under a tree, but the elders decided this would have to be stopped. They had to kill the mother, though they saved her remaining offspring.

Our village also had a "mad woman," though when the villagers called her this, it was with affection and compassion. When I first met her, I thought of my grandmother's sister, Aunt Lena, who had lost a baby when she was young and never seemed to be herself again. Since I was maybe five or six years old, I could remember the times she would become upset and go on at length about something. White hair all awry, a wild look in her eyes, I would hide under the bed until she wore herself out. As I got older and was better able to understand grief and mental illness, my heart ached for her.

Everyone seemed to know the woman in Chiraa. In the afternoons, she would often wander the road in front of our house. Her hair was unkempt, her clothing just rags, and she was covered in what I thought was white paint. She talked to no one in particular but talked aloud all the same. She knew my name and would interrupt herself to wave and shout out a greeting. "Hello, Akosua Broni!" I would respond with a polite wave back, and she would return to whatever spell or prayer had engrossed her that day.

She also taught me about the dangers of photography, a common concept in many cultures. She did not want her picture taken for fear that her spirit would be drawn into the camera — escaping her soul and body through the lens.

Abena assured me that she had a family who cared for her and her well-being.

Sometimes, when Abena was silent, I would be concerned that she was upset with me. I would ask, "Are you mad at me?"

She would tsk in response and add a clipped, "No."

At first, I didn't understand. I just wanted to ensure our relationship was sound.

I laughed when she explained that she thought I was questioning her sanity. I learned instead to say, "Are you angry (or annoyed or disappointed) with me?"

This was a much better way to read the room.

Culture Shock and Chiefs

On July 12, 1975, I wrote home about what I called "a rough patch." There were so many things I was seeing, learning, and doing — and so many people every day, all at once — I sometimes became overwhelmed and homesick. Anthropologists call this "culture shock." Even seasoned travelers can develop it.

I understood that I was living in a very different culture than my own and that others in Chiraa, especially the children, found my novelty interesting. Most had never seen a White woman up close and personal. I was asked several times if there was sun in the United States because I was so "pale" in comparison. Some of the smaller children were shy and even frightened by me. One day, I reached down to pet a stray cat. It stretched from its slumber and seemed to enjoy the scratches. Until it turned its head and saw me. The hair on its back stood up, and the cat squealed and darted off!

Sisters Across the Sea

Letters home via airmail

Culture Shock and Chiefs

The church in Chiraa

I also received a lot of gifts. The fresh bread was my favorite (next to hip beads, of course), and someone once gave me two live chickens. We had to tie sticks to their ankles so that they would not run away. They spent the summer living in the courtyard, and I did not want anyone to kill them for a meal. I suggested we save them for a going-away party, naïvely hoping folks would forget and my chickens could die from old age. Other people brought me pineapples and fresh bananas, so at least I had plenty of my favorite things to eat.

When I got bored, I sometimes would go across the street to the church, which was unlocked most of the time. Inside, a huge pump organ resided at the back that Samuel, a boy in the village, played during Sunday services. He showed me one day how the organ worked. The little piano I knew primarily entailed the first few lines of "Heart and Soul" (or, at least, my best rendition of it) and snippets of some boogie-woogie songs. I taught him these, and he enthusiastically played the rifts repeatedly. It made me miss home ever more.

At the post office, I mailed my letter. The date coincided with an invitation Abena and I had received to visit her schoolteachers in Sunyani. Mrs. Heskett had been instrumental when I first arrived in Ghana, and I was excited to see her again. C.L. and Henry joined us. Mrs. Heskett, a British woman, and her husband, an Italian man, lived in a modern, European-style home. As she prepared a meal, we chatted in the kitchen. I leaned against the kitchen sink, a familiar place for conversations back home (and likely everywhere!). I shared with her the feelings I was having, and she said that she knew how I felt. She, too, had struggled with culture shock five years earlier when she first came to Ghana to teach.

After lunch, we spent the day with the couple, and they invited us to spend the night. It was God, I was sure, who sent Mrs. Heskett and her encouragements at that crucial time. Both C.L. and I were ready to run back to the United States! I wanted to tell Ms. Denshi, the AFS director in Accra, to come get us. Perhaps she had contacted Mrs. Heskett to reach out to us. How did she know? I didn't realize at the time that this, as the idiom goes, wasn't her first "rodeo" even if it was mine. Mrs. Heskett reminded us how privileged we were to have this once-in-a-lifetime opportunity — how kind and understanding our host families were—and that our itinerary was about to pick up again with new travel and sightseeing. Abena's family had even purchased Broni utensils (European cutlery and a teacup for me to use when I had my meals). They prepared food that I could tolerate. They bought me toilet paper for the outhouse. The villagers visited me and came bearing gifts. I needed to be grateful and humble.

And I needed to appreciate the things I took for granted back home. I was sure my family heaved a sigh of relief when a second letter let them know I was beginning to acclimate.

Having C.L. living nearby also helped. We got together as often as we could, taking turns to listen to each other's complaints (as only someone from one's home culture might do) and share our experiences. One time, we were so nostalgic for familiar food that we went to a grocery store in Kumasi and bought a bottle of ketchup. We poured it over our American scrambled eggs and Ghanaian *kelewele* (a spicy fried plantain). I also grumbled about a time Abena and I visited Henry's uncle in Kumasi. We were allowed to stay upstairs at his place. With too much time spent together and me being a pesky little sister, one day I got on C.L.'s nerves. He snapped at me. I went to my room to lick my wounds, sullen at somehow irritating this friend. Later that day, he came to me to make peace. He invited me to go get spicy mutton kabobs, popcorn, and beer at our favorite chophouse, forgetting whatever bee had buzzed our bonnets.

C.L., Abena, Henry, and I frequently traveled to Kumasi—about the distance from Savannah to

Interacting with a chimpanzee at the Kumasi Zoo

Charleston—to explore this "Garden City of West Africa" or catch transportation north or south. Located in the rural rainforest, cocoa was this region's main cash crop, home to many different tribes as well as animals of all varieties.

I enjoyed visiting the Kumasi Zoo. Covered by a luscious tree canopy, it was shady and a relaxing place to spend the day. I could interact with the animals far more intimately than back home—feeding the monkeys an assortment of bananas and talking to the two elephants who always approached when we visited. They liked us, or perhaps it was the treats they knew we had in our pockets. On one occasion, one of the elephants testily swung his long trunk and hit C.L. right in the chest, knocking him back a step. Two days later, we read in the paper that the elephant passed away from old age.

We also met some fellow Bronis at a wood milling camp, one of whom had a pet gorilla called Old Black Joe. He was fascinating to watch. There was a humanity in his eyes, and — unfortunately adopting the bad habits of people — he liked to smoke and drink soda and beer. He would play with the wooden bracelets I wore on my arms, removing them and trying to put them on his feet or his arms. He spent an equal amount of time studying me. He would reach out to clasp my hands in his, and I felt like we somehow connected. In the cage next to him was a baboon with a bright red bottom. He was not very friendly and would throw things that had he collected at us.

Another time in Kumasi, we made a trip to a local hospital — not because we were ill but for a tour. It was big and modern, just not as sanitary as those back home. We visited three wards and met the patients, talking with them about their illnesses. It was like doing rounds as a nurse! In a town farther north, another hospital was newer and better appointed though more modest in size. In a British cottage-style vein, a single floor held patients with various maladies.

Then came an invitation from the Asantehene, *the* chief of the entire Ashanti empire and (coincidentally) Henry's uncle. Every village has a chief. It is a solemn role one commits to for life, and it is very special when anyone — especially someone like me — is summoned to a meeting.

I had the privilege of meeting two chiefs during my stay.

Shortly after I began my life with the Boatengs, I was presented to Chiraa's chief. He was dressed in his noble regalia and sat upright and proud on his royal stool, reminding me of Abena's father. The chief, however, was said to be a centenarian or even older. No one knew for sure. I donned my ever-handy pink dress (thanking my grandmother again in my head for knowing exactly what I would need.) This simple meeting with Chiraa's chief prepared me for the more significant one with the Asantehene.

In Kumasi, we participated in a ceremony as guests of Otumfuo Opoku Ware II, enthroned just five years prior. When the fourteenth Asantehene had passed away, Henry's uncle — then a lawyer and ambassador to Italy — returned home to begin his reign. The fifteenth Asantehene rarely made public appearances, so this was a big deal. The event drew many participants and spectators. Peaches and music entertained the crowd until Otumfuo arrived. He spoke in his native language, traveling through the throng dressed in the finest kente cloth and elevated on a golden seat. People cheered and shouted his name. We bowed as he neared, stopping to greet his nephew. Then, he acknowledged the rest of us, speaking in British English and shaking our hands. I might have curtsied, I don't remember — too awestruck to know what I was doing or saying. It was so special, I thought I might even forget my own name.

One of the special things Abena's father would do — when we weren't off meeting patients or hobnobbing with royalty — is take me to the Techiman Market, an outdoor bazaar as big as a shopping mall and the largest market in Ghana. To get there, we borrowed Senior Brother's Mercedes-Benz and traveled north. Its location made it ac-

Culture Shock and Chiefs

Tetraeder

Otumfuo Opoku Ware II, the fifteenth Asantehene, in 1980

Lapping

Elephants at Mole National Park

cessible to many people, including merchants and customers from neighboring countries, who would come to sell, barter, and buy. Vendors were sectioned off according to the type of goods, and rows of merchandise seemed to repeat forever. I had been to the farmers market on the outskirts of Savannah, but nothing of such size. This "Food Basket of Ghana" was open year-round, Tuesdays through Fridays.

I stayed close to Abena's father as we walked through the rows. He needed to order supplies for his cocoa farm. He would pause here or there, then barter and buy. The vendors took notes after a sale and arranged for goods to be transported and delivered. As we walked through one area that sold dried, salted fish, I wrinkled my face and placed a hand over my mouth and nose. The pungent odor did not lie. Abena's father whipped out a handkerchief and told me to put it under my nose. I graciously took it, thinking it rather chivalrous. He had soaked it in one of my Avon perfumes. One deep breath sent my head spinning, and I almost passed out. Later, I realized that he did not want me to offend the vendors. Being White, I stuck out like a ghostly thumb. I did not mind the smell of the fish nearly as much, setting my face with a pleasant smile.

On one trip, he bought me a necklace with hand-carved bone beads. In the center was a pendant made from ivory — a carving of an elephant. A symbol of strength and power, it reminded me of my elephant friends in Kumasi. It was such a wonderful offering. What did Abena's father see in me that perhaps I didn't recognize in myself? It is one of my life's treasures. I have often contemplated the sacrifice of the real elephant that was needed to create this sacred gift.*

---

*   Africa's elephant population had declined significantly by the 1980s, due primarily to the ivory trade. Ghana, which long had laws aiming to preserve its wildlife, restricted exports in the mid-1920s, though some legal and illegal trade continued in the decades after. In 1989, the Convention on International Trade in Endangered Species secured an agreement to ban the global sale of ivory. While elephant populations have since increased, many countries continue "to lose substantial numbers." Andrew M. Lemieux and Ronald V. Clarke, "The International Ban on Ivory Sales and Its Effects on Elephant Poaching in Africa," *The British Journal of Criminology* 49, no. 4 (July 2009): 451–471; Esmond Martin, "Effective Law Enforcement in Ghana Reduces Elephant Poaching and Illegal Ivory Trade," *Pachyderm*, no. 48 (July–December 2010): 24–32.

Northern Jaunts

We planned a long trip north of Kumasi. Abena had not traveled there before, so it was an adventure we shared for another first. Our original plan was to voyage as far north as Bolgatanga, about ten hours by bus, but time and money ran short. We made it as far as Tamale, a six-hour trek, visiting several points of interest along the way.

Abena and I met up with Henry and C.L. in Kumasi. We stayed with another one of Henry's uncles and his family. Our rooms were on the second floor, while the family's quarters were situated on the first floor at the back. Open to the street was the family bar. During our stay, I sometimes ventured downstairs to help serve beer to the patrons. More than once, I got a pinch on the butt in jest, and beer sales were up.

One of Henry's cousins was a veterinarian, the kind who inspects slaughterhouses for safety issues and cleanliness. He invited us to visit one. Henry and C.L. entered, while Abena and I remained outside. We could hear the buzz of flies even from where we stood. When C.L came out, he looked green in the face. He described what took place on the butcher tables. The blood of the animals drained into troughs along the floor, flowing to some unknown destination. Children worked there alongside their parents. Their job was to clear out the intestines to be repurposed for sausage. Much like home — only our system was automated.

Later, we ate dinner at a local chophouse, roughly constructed of random wood planks and a corrugated tin roof. The food was good and attracted a mix of foreigners — hikers and other travelers on adventures — who had heard about the restaurant through word of mouth. The rich air smelled of careful cooking and deep seasoning when we entered.

The owners, a married couple, were British but decided to retire in Ghana even though their sons stayed in England. The husband had cooked for the British army in his working years and could have long since retired. He enjoyed cooking and meeting new people. We ate some kind of seasoned meat with rice and gravy. By this time, I had stopped asking people to identify what meat came from what animal in any given dish; I no longer cared. If I was hungry and it tasted good, I would eat it. I was learning to enjoy food (and life?) for what it was, living in the moment. We drank a Tata beer to wash it down.

Later that night, we also took in a movie. We saw an Asian kung fu film with English subtitles. Every time a fighting scene occurred, people in the audience yelled "whoosah!" in

Knowledge and Philosophy

An aerial view of Kintampo waterfalls

unison. A group effort to help the fighters as they conquered evil. Just a few months later, *The Rocky Horror Picture Show* would debut in the United States, so I was ready for such moviegoer participation. Who knew audiences would keep coming back, even decades later, just to relive (or experience for the first time) being a part of the musical and belting out songs with "whoosah!" gusto?

Around eleven o'clock that evening, as Abena and I got ready for bed, we heard two people arguing in English in the street below. We assumed they were Bronis, passing through like us. We overheard the woman accuse the man of having

Knowledge and Philosophy
A canopy walkway at Kintampo waterfalls

an affair, and I thought about how common of a conversation this was. Trust and infidelity are worldwide human concerns. We tried to get some sleep. The next day, it was time to go north.

Our first stop of the day was the Kintampo waterfalls, located next to a village of the same name. To reach them, we had to hike into the jungle. Water from Lake Volta — a human-made reservoir that boasts being the largest in the world — flows through the Pumpum River to end up here, three stories high from the bottom. We climbed down nearly two hundred steps, marveling with each footfall the natural beauty. The air was cold and misty, and rainbows shimmered in the sun's rays, arcing through the cascade. I breathed in the sweet petrichor and listened to the soundtrack of Mother Earth: the sound of water falling to the basin below, exotic birds singing in their native tongue, the wind whipping leaves through the fresh air. This was our first experience with a waterfall. We were quiet, not wanting to interrupt: in awe at how close we were to nature and, in a sense, God.

We ate lunch on a flat surface at the bottom of the waterfall and headed back up the way we came. We boarded a bus and rode it to Yeji, a town in central Ghana, west of Kintampo. Here, we caught a ferry to cross the Volta, heading toward Tamale. This was my first time navigating such a large body of water in such a small vessel — packed with a large body of people and various sundries. Abena and I shivered with fright, the river eerie in its depths. Its dark sheen consumed the sun. The boat captain adeptly navigated, slow and steady, around the upstretched arms of the dead trees. Old, dead branches strangely congregated — like outstretched hands reaching to the sky.

Nearby, a man lost hold of his hat, and it tumbled into our wake. Then, we heard a splash.

"Did you see that!?" Abena asked.

To my astonishment, he had jumped overboard to rescue his hat.

"I hope he doesn't drown," Abena said, and I nodded in concern.

"No, look!" I pointed. He swam back portside, and some of the other passengers hauled him on board — hat in his hand. He was greeted with applause and pats on the back. That relaxed us all, and jokes were shared about the experience.

It took less than an hour to reach the other side, but it felt much longer.

Once in Tamale, we had to travel again by land. A motorcoach took us to Larabanga, a town close to Mole National Park. We arrived late in the evening and checked into our hotel. The hotel served Continental food, so there was something familiar for everyone. My room reminded me of the movie *Casablanca*. The bed was soft and cozy, and the ceiling fan sang a soothing song. As I gazed out the hotel window, I realized how long it had been since I had actually seen the night sky. Far away from city lights, it looked three-dimensional, and innumerable stars danced and dazzled me to sleep. Exactly how people — our ancestors — described it long ago. Close enough to touch. Yet still beyond my reach. How could anyone doubt a master creator after seeing such a meticulously crafted scene?

The next day, still exhausted from our journey, we rested and walked about the area. We wanted to be ready for the wonders of one of Ghana's seven national parks. As we wandered, checking out the local scene, we treated ourselves with a homegrown Ghanaian favorite: the GoldenTree Kingsbite Akuafo Bar. This chocolate is beloved by Ghanaians, not least by the farmers since this lemon-flavored chocolate bar is a tribute to them — "the hard-working cocoa farmers in Ghana," as GoldenTree praises, "who produce the priceless beans that are the base ingredient for any good chocolate."

Emmanuel Owusu

Sailing on the River Volta in Ghana

Akuafo is an Akan word for "farmer," and this sumptuous sweet commemorates the "farmers whose hard work and sweat sustain the Ghanaian economy."

That night, I was so excited I almost couldn't sleep. We spent the evening looking up at the stars shining brightly. Brighter than I had ever seen. No earthly lights to minimize their appearance. The Milky Way was a roadway paved in stars!

Rising before dawn, we joined a group of other tourists around five o'clock in the morning. We shared a continental breakfast. Hot local cocoa for me. Abena was so tired, she slept through our alarm and missed the adventure.

And what an adventure it was!

Back home, particularly in New England or places off the West Coast, people go whale-watching. We went elephant-watching.

It was the rainy season, though, and the flourishing vegetation obscured all the favorite watering holes. We crept as close as we dared so as not to be seen. We could hear these majestic creatures but could not see them due to the thick jungle. I was disappointed. I tried to make out gray patches in between the brush, but did not have any luck. I vowed to return one day during the dry season.

Back at the hotel and waiting for our group to return, Abena grabbed a book and went to read beside the pool. She, too, would have an interesting morning — with a serendipitous encounter with an interesting gentleman.

"As I flipped to a new page, I heard someone saying hello," she later told me. "I turned to discover a handsome African American guy standing next to me."

Henry Ramsey Jr. was a law professor, originally from the Carolinas but visiting Ghana for the first time.

"What a small world!" Abena said, explaining how she was hosting a student from Georgia, his neighboring Southern state.

During their conversation, they talked about the Middle Passage and the connections many African Americans had to countries like Ghana — how the two of them might be related and not even know it.

"The story filled me with sadness," Abena confided in me, "but as reserved as I am, I passed no comments. He gave me his card and took my address and said he would write to me when he went back to the States. Or I should write to him?" The chance encounter was a moment that stirred a wistfulness in Abena. But wrong place, wrong time.

When I had returned from the elephant tour, I located Abena by the pool. I wondered who she was talking to.

"Henry, this is my AFS sister," she said, neither of us knowing at the time just how impressive this man was and would continue to become. Sadly, our group was getting ready to leave Larabanga to return to Tamale and back to Chiraa by way of Kumasi.

As promised, Henry did write to Abena after he went back home.

"He says he wants to invite me to the United States as soon as I finish school," Abena told me one day, reading a letter that had traveled all the way from America to Chiraa's post office box number six.

I was skeptical, perhaps because the proposal reminded me of those from "Superman." The next-door neighbor with the seven wives.

"Henry might be married or have a girlfriend who might want to kill you," I joked, using an idiom to underscore that a significant other might not be so keen on the idea.

But Abena, not understanding my humor, took my words to heart. I learned later that she was so frightened that, in her letters to Henry, she avoided showing any interest in visiting the States and eventually stopped writing to him altogether. She lost contact when she later moved to England. I did not recognize the consternation and regret this caused her.

Benny Coffie
Mole National Park in what is now the Savannah region of Ghana

"In November 2014," she recently admitted to me, "I was off sick from work, and I began to roll back the years. I started thinking about Henry and how we met at Mole National Park in 1975. I have always held the idea that spirits of the dead circulate among us — prompting people whom they wish to connect or reconnect. I was strangely motivated to search for him again, so many decades later. From news stories and others I found online, I discovered he had passed away in March of that year, just months before I began looking.

"When I think about Henry, I wonder what might have been between us. I was sad to learn of his death. I couldn't come to terms with what went through his mind concerning me. I gave him mixed signals in my letters. But in fact, all I

NORTHERN JAUNTS

Lapping

Ghanaian huts in the dry season

was trying to do was avoid coming between him and his wife or girlfriend, if he even had one then. I don't think he ever understood. I never explained. May his Soul Rest in Perfect Peace."

As much as I loved Chiraa, even today I sometimes think about these other regions of Ghana and how different one town could be from the next, especially the vegetation and the housing. Northern abodes, more akin to huts, were constructed with a paler type of clay and roofs made of straw. During the dry season, when work is slow, northern communities paint lovely designs on the sides.

On this dizzying jaunt, I purchased so many souvenirs, Abena's mother laughed when I struggled to carry them and teased me for bringing the whole of the North home.

Bredi

All things originate in Africa.

That was Abena's take on life, and it was beginning to look that way to me.

Not only did Ghana produce much of the world's cocoa, some of it came from "Bredi," the Boateng farm that had been in the family for generations.

Located in Dormaa Ahenkro, near the border of Côte d'Ivoire, the farm's name means "work hard to enjoy," and family members and other laborers harvest the crop and sell it to the Ghanaian government for export.

Near the end of my stay, Abena took me to visit Bredi and her father. We invited C. L. and two other AFS students, Liz and Doug, who were as eager as I was to see it. We met up in Kumasi and boarded an already packed mammy wagon. It was an arduous journey, as far as one could go from where we had been living near the midpoint of the country to the border. There were many miles — many miles! — of dusty roads, wedged among laborers and mothers nursing babies, livestock and chickens bound at their feet, and bundles of produce destined for villages along the way. The roof was packed high with whatever would not fit inside. Everyone took turns hanging out of the sides for a few breaths of fresh air.

At least the radio sang out tunes, helping to pass the time as we hummed along to the BBC's greatest hits.

We arrived after a five-hour, bumpy ride, in what seemed the middle of nowhere. Lush, tall, green trees shaded cocoa plants from the harsh sun. In order to flourish, they need a tropical, damp environment, and the tree canopy created another world below.

I was astounded at first sight.

And not just cocoa…but pawpaw, orange trees, plantains and bananas, and wild cocoyam. The farm was big enough to feed Ghana.

There was also a weird little fern growing all over the place, often lining a path. When I touched its leaves, they would close.

"That's the mimosa plant," Abena explained. "Variations of it grow in other parts of the world too. Hunters use it for tracking game. We call it *fedee ne owuo*, which translates to 'better dead than ashamed.'"

Apparently, it has grown in Ghana forever, and during the time when people were being kidnapped and sold into slavery, it helped to save lives as well.

Suyash Dwivedi

The leaves of the Mimosa pudica *plant fold inward when touched*

"It was also used to track slave traders," Abena told us in a quiet, solemn tone. "Villagers knew when they were close by. We have other ferns that close at sundown and open in the mornings. There are similar plants in South America. It makes me wonder if they, too, came from Africa."

We walked around the farm inspecting the cocoa plants. July was the month for a second harvest, so everyone was busy at work. Farmworkers carried machetes to trim back the plants and slice off the pods. It was demanding work. Foliage grows quickly in this environment. Growth time and harvest take four years.

Sisters Across the Sea

Pixabay

Cocoa pods growing in Ghana, and jute sacks filled with processed cocoa beans

One of the workers let us taste fresh cocoa beans straight from the pods. The beans were covered in a white substance. It tasted sweet. The bean was bitter.

Once the pods are opened, the beans are separated and laid out for fermentation and drying in the sun. Then, they are shoveled by hand into burlap bags and stored in a tin roof warehouse right on the farm. The warehouse was where we bedded down at night — looking up at the rafters and feeling the beans shift beneath our bodies as we slept atop the burlap bags.*

---

* Perhaps not so coincidentally, another exchange student from the 1978 cohort, Steven Wallace, created the first "single origin" chocolate bar in 1994. He, too, fell in love with Ghana and its people and documented his adventures and his Omanhene Cocoa Bean Company in the book *Obroni and the Chocolate Factory*.

Coming Together

Abena and Akosua. We were two girls, now women, from different cultures and countries and with different shades to our skin. Sisters from different families, who came to be connected — yet we had always been connected, linked through long-lost lineages that once began in Africa or, as author and poet Margaret Atwood reminds us, as members of the human race.

I grew up in Georgia, a place long steeped in structural racism, where it once was accepted to segregate people and dehumanize neighbors through both language and deed. As a child in Savannah in the 1960s, I remember riding in the family car on a trip uptown to Broughton Street. There were no seatbelt laws then, so I was standing up and leaning over the back of the seat. I noticed a group of people gathered at a bus stop. Confused about racial terms that were common at the time, I wondered aloud: "If those are 'colored peo-

AFS'er Home

Josie Mooney

Josie Mooney returned in September from a two month stay in Ghana, Africa as an exchange student with the American Field Service Americans Abroad Program.

She and 21 other students were selected from the United States to visit Ghana. Josie lived with a family in the bush section. Her African home was in Chiraa, a small village.

"I didn't think I could stick it out because it was so different," said Josie. Telegrams flew on the wires between New York, Savannah, and Chiraa, but Josie decided to stay. "I realized the importance of experiencing an entirely different life-style."

Josie's experiences included teaching Ghanian children American games and songs of their homeland. She learned the language of the Brongs and Anafo tribes.

Josie summarized the whole trip by saying, "My A.F.S. experience taught me a lot. I'm really glad I had the chance to experience what I did."

Ambulance Service

The American Field Service has been active at Jenkins for three years. It originated in 1914 as a voluntary ambulance service to help the French care for their wounded soldiers. After WW II, A.F.S. expanded its efforts to promote a more peaceful world.

Herschel V. Jenkins High School newspaper

Josie Mooney reflects on her time in Ghana

ple,' then where are the other colors?" In my childlike mind, I envisioned the variegated rainbow of a box of Crayola Crayons — and along the lines of the sixty-four pack that had just been introduced.

Abena first met a White person when she was four. He worked in the timber industry and was nicknamed "Kwesi

Aya" (a fernlike boy born on Sunday). She and her friends would watch as he cooked cocoyam on an open fire, opened it, and ate it. They often played on the timber — a place to sit and talk or test one's balance by walking and wobbling along the beams. He was learning to speak Twi and would shoo them away when he needed to load the timber and haul it away.

We have come a long way since then, and perhaps the world has too. But there remains much work to be done and many minds and hearts to be healed.

This is one reason why Abena established a primary school and orphanage in Sunyani that teaches the basic educational requirements to attend secondary school. She imbues the curriculum with a multilayered understanding of intelligence: not merely the ability to learn academic concepts and skills and apply such knowledge appropriately but also vocational proficiencies, financial planning, cultural and emotional competence, care and respect for others (from infants to elders), and curiosity and creativity. She has dedicated her life to providing children with opportunities to explore their own areas of interest and carve their own paths.

In 2008, I celebrated my birthday by taking a trip to Chiraa to visit the family and Abena's school. I spent time with the students, teaching them the same silly songs I had shared as a teen.

In 2015, Abena and I bought a cashew farm. We call it the "Two Sisters Farm" or "Abusua Ahokeka," which means "family." Profits from the farm support the school and

Love Divine International, an orphanage and school in Sunyani, Ghana

Abena's eventual retirement. Our long-term goal is to expand the school to be a campus of learning and growth.

Whether people are sisters or strangers, we have come to believe that communicating our experiences, encouraging each other's dreams, and sharing food around a table can make all the difference.

Abena has long made me this special beef dish. When we were teenagers, we would walk together to the market in Chiraa and buy some chunks of beef, along with rice, tomatoes, and a few other things. When we got home, she would place the beef on a cassava leaf that acted like tin foil or plastic wrap (yet far more ecologically friendly!) to keep it fresh for a day. Then she'd turn it into Ghanaian *jollof*, a spicy rice stew that filled both my stomach and my heart. I could never seem to make it back home, not like hers.

In my attempts, I often failed. But at least I tried.

We continue to learn as individuals and to learn together. We have even found commonality in boiled peanuts!

As Nelson Mandela believed and practiced: "Education is the most powerful weapon which you can use to change the world."

He also said: "It always seems impossible until it is done."

Acknowledgments

We would first like to thank you, the reader, for choosing to engage with our story. We have been discussing the construction of this book for many years and decided — before we grew too old to remember — that we needed to dedicate time to weave our stories together in some orderly fashion. With apologies for any errors or omissions, this is the tale of two young women, an ocean apart, who shared an adventure and became sisters.

As with raising children, few worthwhile undertakings succeed without the help of a village.

Several people read this book in its rough draft. They made corrections, asked for clarifications and expansions on subjects, and tried to ensure the final product would be funny and tastefully done. We appreciate their eagle-eyed efforts and attention: Gabrielle Larochelle (her first editing job), Jim and Sarah Ford, Felicia Johnson, and Patricia Reed.

And speaking of sisters...a word of thanks to several longtime friends of Jo's: Tina Smith (from high school), Lexie Bowen (a colleague while working in Germany for Enterprise and later in Ozark, Alabama), and Raye Maddox (originally from Canada and now residing in Dothan, Alabama). Each sister entered Jo's life at a time she needed them. They believe in her — and her crazy ideas — and have offered Jo unconditional support.

Additionally, a special thanks needs to be said to Tina Varick, who fostered an awakening while parts of this book were being written — an awakening that will continue until the time has come to leave this mortal coil.

Jo's husband also has long been the "one holding tight to the kite's string." When Jo rambles around the house muttering, "If I could only…(fill in the blank)," he interrupts this lamenting and responds, "Just do it," and then contemplates and offers suggestions for making ideas better. He has proven to be a great mentor and muse.

Though necessity often is the mother of invention, mothers are crucial in both community-building and creative endeavors. Jo's mother saved her letters, postcards, and other mementos from so many decades ago — which Jo found in a box after her mother passed in 2014. These provided the foundation of this book.

Last and always first…without God, none of this would be possible.

Abena and Akosua agree. Amen.

About the Authors

Agnes (Abena) Boateng is a lecturer at Richmond Upon Thames College and the author of the textbook *Combined English and Maths*. She has lived in the same flat in London for more than thirty years. She has one son and five grandchildren. In 2006, she founded Love Divine International, an orphanage and school in Sunyani, Ghana. She began with one student and now supports more than one hundred who attend regularly. Enrollment has outgrown the location, and she is hoping to expand.

Jo (Akosua) Williams is a social worker who owns her own counseling business in the town where she has lived for the past two decades with her forever husband. Between the two of them, they have six adult children. She has traveled the world some and written as part of her career. She enjoys writing, whether with an educational goal in mind or simply for fun. This is her first book.

Together, they own an almond farm in Ghana.

monte ceceri

In the early 1500s, it was from the heights of Monte Ceceri — otherwise known as "Swan Mountain" — in Fiesole, Italy, that inventor and artist Leonardo da Vinci let soar one of his experimental flying machines.

Envisioning a future where such fantastical creations would one day become reality, Leonardo desired to fill the world with awe-inspiring inventions and ideas.

Like its namesake's Renaissance roots, Monte Ceceri Publishers supports avant-garde writers whose works challenge current perspectives, inspire new paths, and speak to a modern-day humanism.

Based in Savannah, Georgia, Monte Ceceri is an independent publisher of books that raise issues of social, cultural, and philosophical interest, cross disciplinary boundaries, and facilitate cross-cultural dialogue through effective and engaging writing.

Monte Ceceri Publishers, LLC

www.ingramcontent.com/pod-product-compliance
Lightning Source LLC
Chambersburg PA
CBHW061800070526
44586CB00023B/2655